MW01290918

Bread Machine Cookbook

Simple and Easy Gluten-Free Recipes
for Home DIY Baking Using Your
Bread Maker

Sierra A. May

Bluesource And Friends

This book is brought to you by Bluesource And Friends, a happy book publishing company.

Our motto is **"Happiness Within Pages"**

We promise to deliver amazing value to readers with our books.

We also appreciate honest book reviews from our readers.

Connect with us on our Facebook page

www.facebook.com/bluesourceandfriends and stay tuned to our latest book promotions and free giveaways.

Don't forget to claim your FREE books!

Brain Teasers:

https://tinyurl.com/karenbrainteasers

Harry Potter Trivia:

https://tinyurl.com/wizardworldtrivia

Sherlock Puzzle Book (Volume 2)

https://tinyurl.com/Sherlockpuzzlebook2

Also check out our best seller book

"67 Lateral Thinking Puzzles"

https://tinyurl.com/thinkingandriddles

Table of Contents

Introduction

Welcome to my book, *Bread Machine Cookbook: Simple and Easy Gluten-Free Recipes for Home DIY Baking Using Your Bread Machine*!

So you decided to take the big step and try your hand at baking gluten-free bread. You go to the internet and come up with a bunch of recipes—all talking about the same thing. If it is your first time, it can be overwhelming at first. But then again, nobody is perfect at anything the first time! That is why this recipe book comes in handy; it comes not only with recipes but also with a few tips and tricks that can help you learn along the way.

The next chapters detail the delicious and easy recipes that you can use with your bread machine. You can be a first-timer, with no idea on how to bake, or you can be an advanced baker looking to expand your skills. This recipe book will fit whichever skill level you are at in baking. Ingredients will be discussed and clearly given, the procedures will be detailed, and all that you need to make sure is to follow the steps. It even has nutritional information so that you know what you are consuming.

If you are unable to eat gluten, don't fret. While it requires a bit of an adjustment on your part, the good news it—you have a chance to discover healthy alternatives which can benefit you in the long run. These alternatives are still as healthy, delicious, and easy to prepare so that you will be more encouraged to keep up with eating gluten-free food.

While of course there are plenty of packaged gluten-free foods including cookies, bread, pies, and more, why not enjoy them fresh from the oven? That taste of freshly baked bread just cannot compare. As you go through the recipes in this book, you will fall in love with the process of baking.

Before you begin baking, let go of any expectations you may have about baking. Up to this point, you have most likely been baking a certain way for your whole life. When individuals begin baking with gluten-free ingredients, the change of flours can be a difficult task. Due to this factor, letting go of expectations will prevent you from feeling disappointed.

This is your first time baking gluten-free bread dough? It would look different from what the traditional dough would look like. It may even feel a little differently to the touch. But that is the uniqueness of gluten-free bread. It should have the denseness and thickness of pancake batter to ensure that it will bake well. Stick to the recipe, for now, and follow everything to the dot. After some practice (and failures) you will find that you can perfect a loaf without even looking at the recipes! It all takes time and patience on your part. During preparation, you might be tempted to make adjustments if you feel that the dough you are working on doesn't feel right. It may be too dry, so you add water. It may be too wet, so you add more flour. Don't jump the gun yet. Learn and master the basics, then if you feel comfortable with the basic process, you can tweak it according to your liking.

When you are ready, you can move onto the first chapter. There, we will be discussing different flours to use when you begin using your bread machine. For many, this is where they get stuck with baking. For regular baking and cooking, there is one "magic" flour used in almost every recipe. While there are a few recipes you can use one kind of flour in, you will have to combine two to three flours to make gluten-free baking work! In the chapter to follow, I will guide you through the different types of flours to use and how to use them.

Now, let's get ready to bake!

Chapter One: Gluten-Free Ingredients

As mentioned earlier, getting used to your new gluten-free ingredients may be the hardest change for you. I am going to let you in on a little secret. Most baked goods are going to be even better without gluten! If you think back to your old baking ways, you may remember an instruction warning you to not over-stir. Have you ever thought about what would happen if you do? When you over-stir ingredients with gluten, this activates the gluten and makes the cake (or whatever you are baking) tough! When you don't have gluten in the first place, your bread and treats come out nice and fluffy! Below, I will provide you with some information about some of the best gluten-free alternative flours you can use while using your bread machine!

Gluten-Free Flour Alternatives

For those of you just starting out, gluten-free baking can sound incredibly daunting. As you are probably aware, gluten is the protein that is found in products including barley, wheat, and rye. If you read a food item with unbleached, refined flour, or wheat in the title, it probably contains gluten.

Luckily for all of us, there are many gluten-free flours that are readily available at our favorite stores. Many companies are hopping on the gluten-free bandwagon to help individuals who are gluten intolerant, gluten sensitive, and who are Celiac. For some, you may not even be able to tell the difference in your baked goods, which is good for those of us trying to cook for a family of picky eaters!

1. Almond Flour

   You probably could have guessed this, but almond flour is made by grinding almonds into a coarse powder. Almond flour can be made using almonds without skin or blanched almonds. Almond flour is an excellent alternative as it is low in carbohydrates and high in fiber. If you are diabetic or trying to avoid carbohydrates in your diet, almond flour is an excellent choice. Almond flour is best used in recipes such as cookies and quick bread. If you are trying to make a cake with your bread machine, you will want to use finer almond flour.

2. Oat Flour

   Oat Flour is another popular gluten-free alternative for flour. While oats themselves are gluten-free, you will need to be sure that they are not cross contaminated when they are blended. You will want to be especially careful if you have Celiac disease. If you are really crafty, oat flour is incredibly easy to make on your own! All you have to do is place the oats in a food processor and pulse until you achieve the desired texture. While these oats do have a mild taste, they typically have a dense texture. Oat flour is great for cookies, cakes, and pancakes! Oat flour also provides an excellent amount of protein and fiber. If you are looking to lower cholesterol and risk of heart disease, oat flour is an excellent choice for you.

3. Coconut Flour

Coconut products are becoming more and more popular on the market; it is no surprise that coconut flour is becoming more popular as well. Coconut flour is created from the inside meat of the coconut being dried and ground into a fine powder. This specific type of flour has healthy fats, high in protein, and low in carbohydrates. If you have a nut allergy, wheat allergy, or diabetes, coconut flour will be an excellent alternative for your baking needs. The one thing you should know before purchasing coconut flour is that it is typically sweet from the coconut. It also has a strong scent of coconut and typically has a finer texture compared to other flours. If you do not like coconut, this taste can be hard to mask. However, this flour is excellent for bread, brownies, and cinnamon buns.

4. Brown Rice Flour

    Rice flour is by far one of the most popular flour alternatives to using in gluten-free baking. There are several different types including white rice flour, brown rice flour, and even sweet rice flour. The texture of these flours, while extremely fine is also kind of gritty. On top of this benefit, the rice flour is typically mild in taste and can be mixed into several baking products. This type of flour is best used in bread, brownies, pancakes, and cakes. Rice flour will typically be the cheapest alternative flour you will find on the market.

5. Gluten-Free Baking Mix

    If you do not feel like messing around with all different flours, gluten-free baking flour will be perfect for you. This is a specific mixture if a combination of flours and grains that are created to mimic all-purpose flour. This type of baking mix can be used one for one, meaning that a recipe that requires one cup of all-purpose flour can use one cup of the gluten-free flour mix. The good news is that this baking mixed can be used in all different types of gluten-free baking but typically will cost you a bit more.

6. Sorghum Flour

If you are like me, you probably have not heard much about sorghum flour. This type of flour if a gluten-free grain that is soft in texture and sweet in flavor. There are many cereal grains that use sorghum flour. This grain is high in protein, fiber, and is an excellent source of antioxidants. Typically, this flour will be used in recipes for muffins, bread, and pizzas. Sorghum flour is also used in beer, but this is a book for baking, not beer!

7. Buckwheat Flour

While buckwheat is sometimes associated with gluten, buckwheat comes from a completely different botanical family from wheat. This type of flour is excellent for those with high blood pressure and type two diabetes. Buckwheat typically has a nutty flavor and is excellent for making bread. You will want to make sure the flour has not been exposed to nuts during manufacturing if you also have a nut allergy.

8. Quinoa Flour

   If you are looking to make your bread and baked goods a bit healthier, quinoa flour will be an excellent choice. Generally, this type of flour is high in protein and is known to be the healthiest of all of the grains. If you are vegetarian or vegan, this flour can provide you with the amino acids you need in your diet. It can also help if you have high blood pressure or high blood sugar levels. Typically, quinoa flour has a nutty flavor that pairs well with waffles, pancakes, bread, and other baked goods.

9. Xanthan Gum

   Before we move onto the fun part of baking, you must learn that xanthan gum is going to be your new best friend. You may not realize this, but many of the gluten-free flour alternatives lack a binding agent. A binding agent is helpful to hold your food together, much like gluten does when used in baking and cooking. The moment you remove gluten, all mixtures will typically crumble and fall apart. Xanthan gum is made from lactose, sucrose, and glucose that have been fermented from a specific bacterium. When this is added to liquid, it creates a gum and is used with gluten-free baking. As a general guide, you will be using one teaspoon of xanthan gum for one cup of gluten-free flour that you use. For some mixes, this gum is already added so when you are baking; you will always want to check the ingredient label. It should be noted that xanthan gum can be expensive, but it will last you a long time.

If you have an allergy to xanthan gum, you can find ways around it. Instead, you can try using psyllium husks, ground flaxseeds, or ground chia seeds. Psyllium can be sold in full husks or in powder. As you bake more, you will soon find what works for you, and what doesn't! For a quick reference of flours, you can use while baking gluten-free, refer to the list below.

10. Arrowroot Flour

Arrowroot flour and starch are excellent alternatives for cornstarch. Unlike corn, this plant is not genetically modified like cornstarch and acts as a thickening agent. If you are looking to make your cakes and bread softer, arrowroot flour will be the way to go. The great news is that arrowroot flour has no flavor and will not overwhelm the flavors of your bread. This flour is also excellent for puddings, soups, and sauces as well.

11. Bean Flours

Bean flours are another alternative that you can use. It is similar with arrowroot or cornstarch which can be used as a thickener. Available kinds of bean flours are the Soy Bean, Garbanzo, and the Fava Beans.

12. Nut Flours

Nut flours are derived from a variety of nuts which are raw and/or dried and have been ground to a fine powder. Nut flours bring texture and moisture due to the oils inherent in the nuts themselves and bring about a rich taste. Notable nut flour variants are – hazelnuts, coconut, chestnut, and the popular kind, the almond flours.

13. White Flours

This type of flour comes from White Rice, Tapioca, Sweet Rice, Potato, Cornstarch, and Arrowroot.

14. Whole Grain Flours

Whole grain flours come from Teff, Sweet Potato, Sorghum, Quinoa, Oats, Millet, Mesquite, Corn, Buckwheat, and Brown Rice

Before you begin baking, I want to remind you that more than likely, you are going to make mistakes! You cannot expect yourself to suddenly become a master-baker just because you picked up one book!

As mentioned earlier, you are probably used to baking one way and one way only. I invite you to return to a beginner's mindset. As you learn the new textures of your flours and doughs, expect to bake some ugly loaves of bread first. Eventually, you will get the hang of it and enjoy your delicious meals! When you think about it, the worst that can happen is a few bad, baked goods! I invite you to push past these failures and try again.

Whenever you make a mistake try to make a note what part of the recipe you had trouble with. Was it with the measurements? Was it with the time of baking? Or maybe how you prepared the dough? These things tend to be a little specific and it is pertinent that you would stick to the recipe at first, perfect it, and then try tweaking the recipe to fit your palate. Of course, I encourage you to put variations depending on your preference as what you enjoy may be different from what others enjoy. Start with the basics then move forward. Eventually, you will get the hang of it!

When you are prepared, let's get baking.

Chapter Two: Gluten-Free Bread Recipes

If you purchased this book because you recently found out that you are sensitive to gluten and wheat products, you are holding the perfect resource. On a positive note, with this sensitivity you have with gluten and/or wheat products, you are not alone. There are approximately 18 million in the US who are affected with the same sensitivity, which is why this book would be a wonderful resource for anyone who needs to make the switch to gluten-free due to health reasons

I will be providing you with several bread recipes you can recreate in your own bread machine. Your bread machine will do all of the work for you, and by the end, you will have a delicious treat for your whole family. The recipes included in this book are meant to be used with the latest model of the bread machine. It should automatically knead and bake the bread for you.

In order to do this, you will need to select the manual cycle to prepare the dough for you in the provided bread machine pan. Once the kneading cycle is finished, you will want to use your hands to transfer the dough to a clean workspace that has been dusted with gluten-free flour. I suggest wetting your hands before touching the dough to avoid it sticking to you. Once the dough is in place, punch the dough down and cover so you can allow it to rest for thirty to forty-five minutes. By the end of this time period, the dough should at least double in size.

At this point, you will transfer the dough into a greased pan and bake the bread in a heated oven of 350 degrees. Typically, the bread will take anywhere from twenty to twenty-five minutes to bake. By the end, the top of the bread should be a nice, golden-brown color. You should also be able to insert a toothpick into your bread and have it come out clean when you remove it. When you are ready, start up the bread machine, and we can begin!

Apple Pie Bread

Time: Three Hours

Yields: One and a Half Pound Loaf

Ingredients:

- Apple Pie Filling (1.25 C.)
- Xanthan Gum (2 t.)
- Potato Starch (1 C.)
- Gluten-free Almond Flour (2 C.)
- Baking Powder (.50 t.)
- Dry Active Yeast (2 t.)
- Apple Cider Vinegar (1 T.)
- Egg Whites (2)
- Honey (3 T.)
- Olive Oil (.25 C.)
- Buttermilk (1.25 C.)

Directions:

1. To begin this recipe, you will want to place all of the ingredients from above into your bread machine. Be sure that you grease the pan well before putting everything in.

2. Once in place, you will want to select sweet bread, quick bread, bake, normal cycle, or basic cycle depending on your model. Once you have done this,

you will then select the crust color to be either light or medium. When you have done this, you can press start and begin baking the bread.

3. When the machine has reached the last kneading cycle, you will want to check the consistency of your dough. By the last cycle, the dough should be wet and thick. If the dough feels it's too wet, make an adjustment by adding a tablespoon of flour, and you can always add one tablespoon of flour at a time. You will continue adding flour until your dough is firm. On the other hand, if the dough feels dry, you can also add one tablespoon of water at a time.

4. Once the baking cycle of the bread machine is finished, you will want to turn the machine off and remove the pan. Allow the bread to cool for a bit and enjoy!

Nutritional Information:

Calories: 100

Carbs: 20g

Fats: 18g

Proteins: 2g

Almond and Dried Berry Bread

Time: Three Hours

Yields: One and a Half Pound Loaf

Ingredients:

- Dried Cranberries (.50 C.)
- Toasted Almonds (.50 C.)
- Salt (1 t.)
- Xanthan Gum (2 t.)
- Potato Starch (1 C.)
- Gluten-free Almond Flour (2 C.)
- Sugar (4 T.)
- Dry Active Yeast (2 t.)
- Baking Powder (.50 t.)
- Apple Cider Vinegar (1 t.)
- Egg Whites (2)
- Olive Oil (.25 C.)
- Unsweetened Milk (1.25 C.)

Directions:

1. To begin, you will want to place all of the ingredients from the list above into your bread maker. Before you place the ingredients, be sure to follow the instructions provided with the bread machine and

grease the pan well to avoid anything sticking and/or burning while you are making your bread.

2. Next, you will select one of the following cycles according to your own model: sweet bread, quick bread, bake, normal, or basic cycle. Once this is done, you can select either light crust color or a medium crust color. When you have selected your preference, you can press the start button and begin to bake your bread.

3. On the last cycle, you will want to check the consistency of the dough that you are creating. At this point, the dough should be thick and still slightly wet. Remember that your gluten-free dough is not going to look like the dough that you are used to. At this point, if the dough feels it's too wet, make an adjustment by adding a tablespoon of flour, you can add a tablespoon of flour one at a time. If the dough feels dry, try adding a tablespoon of water until you achieve a slightly firm dough.

4. When the cycle is finished, turn your machine off and remove the bread pan. Allow the bread to cool on a wire rack for ten to fifteen minutes, and then you can enjoy!

Nutritional Information:

Calories: 150

Carbs: 5g

Fats: 11g

Proteins: 7g

Banana Nut Bread

Time: Three Hours

Yields: One and a Half Pound Loaf

Ingredients:

- Chopped Walnuts (.50 C.)
- Salt (1 t.)
- Xanthan Gum (2 t.)
- Potato Starch (1 C.)
- Gluten-free Almond Flour (2 C.)
- Sugar (2 T.)
- Dry Active Yeast (2 t.)
- Baking Powder (.50 t.)
- Apple Cider Vinegar (1 T.)
- Banana (.75 C.)
- Egg Whites (2)
- Olive Oil (.25 C.)
- Honey (.50 C.)
- Unsweetened Milk (1.25 C.)

Directions:

1. Before you begin baking your banana nut bread, you will want to place the ingredients from the list above into your bread machine according to the directions provided. Be sure you grease the pan well before

placing the ingredients to avoid any sticking or burning.

2. Once all of the ingredients from the list above are in place, you will select one of the following cycles depending on your bread machine model: sweet bread, quick bread, bake, normal, or basic cycle. When the cycle is selected, you should have the option to create either a light or medium crust color. After you have made your selections, press the start button and begin to bake your bread.

3. In the last kneading cycle, you will want to check the consistency of the dough you have just created. By this point, the bread should be thick and wet. If it is too wet, feel free to add more flour as needed. You will want to do this a tablespoon at a time to avoid the dough becoming too firm. The same stands if the dough is too dry, add one tablespoon of water until the desired consistency is achieved.

4. Once the cycle is finished, you can turn the bread machine off, remove the pan, and allow the bread to cool. This bread makes an excellent breakfast or treat after dinner!

Nutritional Information:

Calories: 141

Carbs: 30g

Fats: 7g

Proteins: 3g

Cheese and Herb Bread

Time: Three Hours

Yields: One and a Half Pound Loaf

Ingredients:

- Dried Oregano (.75 t.)
- Dried Basil (.75 t.)
- Dried Marjoram (1 t.)
- Grated Parmesan Cheese (2 T.)
- Salt (1 t.)
- Xanthan Gum (2 t.)
- Potato Starch (1 C.)
- Gluten-free Almond Flour (2 C.)
- Sugar (2 T.)
- Dry Active Yeast (2 t.)
- Baking Powder (.50 t.)
- Apple Cider Vinegar (1 T.)
- Egg Whites (2)
- Olive Oil (.25 C.)
- Warm Water (1.25 C.)

Directions:

1. Before we begin, you may note that this recipe requires warm water as opposed to milk. This will be a very important factor to achieve the light and fluffy

bread out of the following ingredients. When you are ready, carefully place all of the ingredients above into your bread machine.

2. When all of the ingredients are in place, you will first be selecting the cycle. Depending on your model, you will be choosing the white bread, quick bread, bake, normal, or basic cycle. At this point, you can also decide if you want a light or medium crust color. When these two steps have been completed, press the start button and begin to bake your bread.

3. As always, you will want to check the consistency of your bread at the last cycle. The dough for your bread should be thick and wet. If it is too wet, add in more flour and if the dough feels dry, add more water. Be sure to complete both of these tasks one tablespoon at a time to avoid having the dough turning too thick or thin again.

4. When the cycle is complete, turn the machine off and remove the pan. You should allow the bread to cool for ten to fifteen minutes before enjoying. This cheese and herb bread makes an excellent start to any meal or can be enjoyed alone! There is no judgment here.

Nutritional Information:

Calories: 150

Carbs: 9g

Fats: 3g

Proteins: 4g

Chocolate Chip Bread

Time: Three Hours

Yields: One and Half Pound Loaf

Ingredients:

- Salt (1 t.)
- Xanthan Gum (2 t.)
- Potato Starch (1 C.)
- Gluten-free Almond Flour (2 C.)
- Sugar (2 T.)
- Dry Active Yeast (2 t.)
- Baking Powder (.50 t.)
- Apple Cider Vinegar (1 T.)
- Egg Whites (2)
- Olive Oil (.25 C.)
- Warm Water (1.25 C.)

Directions:

1. Your first step to making warm and delicious chocolate chip bread is to place all of the ingredients from the list above minus your chocolate chips. It may

be easiest to add in the dry ingredients first and then gently pour in the wet ingredients. As always, you will want to be sure that the bread pan of your bread machine is greased to avoid sticking or burning.

2. Once everything is in place, you will select a cycle depending on your bread machine model. This cycle may be labeled sweet bread, quick bread, bake, normal, or a basic cycle. When you have found the cycle, you will also be selecting a light or a medium crust color. When these two steps are complete, you can press the start button and begin breaking your bread.

3. During the last cycle of kneading, go ahead and check the consistency of the dough. By this point, you should have a dough that is fairly thick, but still wet. If needed, adjust the dough with either a tablespoon of water or flour until you get the desired consistency. Remember that gluten-free dough is going to be different from what you are used to.

4. Five minutes before the cycle ends, you will want to add in the chocolate chips. When the cycle is complete, turn the machine off and remove the bread pan from the machine. Allow the bread to cool slightly

and enjoy the warm, gooey chocolate chip bread! The family is sure to love this recipe.

Nutritional Information:

Calories: 190

Carbs: 20g

Fats: 10g

Proteins: 5g

Cinnamon Raisin Bread

Time: Three Hours

Yields: One and Half Pound Loaf

Ingredients:

- Raisins (1 C.)
- Ground Cinnamon (1 t.)
- Salt (1 t.)
- Xanthan Gum (2 t.)
- Potato Starch (1 C.)
- Gluten-free Almond Flour (2 C.)
- Sugar (2 T.)
- Dry Active Yeast (2 t.)
- Baking Powder (.50 t.)
- Apple Cider Vinegar (1 T.)
- Egg Whites (2)
- Honey (2 T.)
- Olive Oil (.25 C.)
- Warm Water (1.25 C.)

Directions:

1. To begin making your delicious cinnamon raisin bread, you will first want to grease the bread pan well to help avoid sticking or burning during the baking process. Once this step is complete, carefully add in

the dry ingredients from the list above except for the one cup of raisins. When everything is in place, pour in your liquid ingredients.

2. When all of the ingredients are in place, you will want to select a cycle depending on the model of your bread machine. It will be either sweet bread, quick bread, bake, normal, or basic cycle. Once the cycle is selected, you will also want to select either a light or medium crust color before you press start.

3. As the bread machine hits the final kneading cycle, you will want to take a few moments to check the consistency of your dough. For cinnamon raisin bread, the dough should be fairly thick but still wet. If it does not look like this, add either a tablespoon of water or flour depending on what you need at the moment.

4. In the last five minutes of the cycle, this is the point you will add in the cup of raisins. Finally, when the cycle is over, turn the bread machine off and remove the bread pan. Allow the bread to cool for ten to fifteen minutes before consuming. This cinnamon raisin bread is perfect for spicing up any breakfast!

Nutritional Information:

Calories: 90

Carbs: 14g

Fats: 2g

Proteins: 3g

Coconut Bread

Time: Three Hours

Yields: One and a Half Pound Loaf

Ingredients:

- Salt (1 t.)
- Xanthan Gum (2 t.)
- Potato Starch (1 C.)
- Gluten-free Almond Flour (2 C.)
- Shredded Coconut (.33 C.)
- Sugar (2 T.)
- Dry Active Yeast (2 t.)
- Baking Powder (.50 t.)
- Apple Cider Vinegar (1 T.)
- Egg Whites (2)
- Coconut Extract (1.50 t.)
- Olive Oil (.25 C.)
- Unsweetened Coconut Milk (1.25 C.)

Directions:

1. To start, all you have to do is place all of the ingredients from the list above into the pan of your bread machine. Be sure that you grease the pan well, or you will regret it later as you try to scrape your bread from the pan.

2. Once everything is in place, select the cycle that is on your bread machine. It may say sweet bread, quick bread, and bake, normal, or basic cycle. You will also choose either a light or medium crust color at this point. When you have pressed all of the right buttons, press start and get one step closer to this delicious bread!

3. During the last cycle of kneading, take a few minutes to check the consistency of the dough. Remember that while you do want the dough to be thick, it should still be slightly wet in order for it to bake properly. Add water or flour to achieve a slightly firm dough. Once this step is done, complete the baking cycle.

4. When the baking cycle is finished, turn your machine off and remove the bread from the pan. Allow the bread to cool for ten to fifteen minutes, and then you can enjoy it.

Nutritional Information:

Calories: 180

Carbs: 35g

Fats: 4g

Proteins: 4g

Dill and Cottage Cheese Bread

Time: Three Hours

Yields: One and a Half Pound Loaf

Ingredients:

- Cottage Cheese (.75 C.)
- Dill Seed (1 T.)
- Dried Onion, Minced (1 t.)
- Salt (1 t.)
- Xanthan Gum (2 t.)
- Potato Starch (1 C.)
- Gluten-free Almond Flour (2 C.)
- Sugar (2 T.)
- Dry Active Yeast (2 t.)
- Baking Powder (.50 t.)
- Apple Cider Vinegar (1 T.)
- Egg Whites (2)
- Olive Oil (.25 C.)
- Warm Water (1.25 C.)

Directions:

1. If you are looking for a more savory bread, this dill and cottage cheese bread should cure your cravings. To start off, be sure that you grease the bread pan well. This will help avoid any sticking or burning

during the baking process. When you are ready, carefully place all of the dry ingredients followed by the wet ingredients into your bread pan.

2. When all of the ingredients from the list above are placed in the pan, select the proper cycle. Depending on your bread machine, it will say one of the following: white bread, quick bread, bake, normal, or basic cycle. Once you have selected the proper cycle, you will also want to choose to create either a light or medium crust color. When you are ready, press start and begin the baking process.

3. During the last cycle, be sure to check the consistency of the dough. At this point, you will want a thick but slightly wet dough. If it does not look as it should, feel free to add water or flour, depending on which you need. When you are happy with the final product, allow the cycle to finish baking your delicious bread.

4. Once the bread is cooked through, turn the machine off and carefully remove your loaf of bread from the pan. You will want to allow the bread to cool on a wire rack for ten to fifteen minutes. Enjoy!

Nutritional Information:

Calories: 140

Carbs: 25g

Fats: 2g

Proteins: 7g

Flaxseed and Sunflower Seed Bread

Time: Three Hours

Yields: One and a Half Pound Loaf

Ingredients:

- Sunflower Seeds (.50 C.)
- Flax Seeds (.50 C.)
- Salt (1 t.)
- Xanthan Gum (2 t.)
- Potato Starch (1 C.)
- Gluten-free Almond Flour (2 C.)
- Sugar (2 T.)
- Dry Active Yeast (2 t.)
- Baking Powder (.50 t.)
- Apple Cider Vinegar (1 T.)
- Egg Whites (2)
- Olive Oil (.25 C.)
- Warm Water (1.25 C.)

Directions:

1. Sometimes, plain bread can get rather boring. This sunflower and flax seed bread will add some flavor to your pallet. To begin, you will just need to grease your bread pan and place the ingredients from the list

above in. At this point, you will want to leave out the sunflower seeds.

2. When everything is in place, it is now time to select the proper setting according to your model of bread machine. The setting will be either white bread, quick bread, bake, normal, or basic cycle. You will also want to select either light or medium crust color. When all of the decisions have been made, go ahead and press start!

3. Once the bread machine is in the final cycle, check the dough consistency. For this specific bread, the dough should be wet and thick. If needed, add flour to make the dough drier. If the dough feels dry, add in a tablespoon or so of extra water. By the end, the dough should be slightly firm. When the dough consistency is achieved, add in the sunflower seeds and finish the cycle.

4. Finally, turn the machine off and remove your baked bread from the pan. Once this step is complete, allow the bread to cool on a wire rack and then enjoy it.

Nutritional Information:

Calories: 90

Carbs: 19g

Fats: 2g

Proteins: 4g

Jalapeno Corn Bread

Time: Three Hours

Yields: One and a Half Pound Loaf

Ingredients:

- Chopped Jalapeno Pepper (1 T.)
- Corn (.75 C.)
- Cornmeal (.33 C.)
- Salt (1 t.)
- Xanthan Gum (2 t.)
- Potato Starch (1 C.)
- Gluten-free Almond Flour (2 C.)
- Sugar (2 T.)
- Dry Active Yeast (2 t.)
- Baking Powder (.50 t.)
- Apple Cider Vinegar (1 T.)
- Egg Whites (2)
- Olive Oil (.25 C.)
- Warm Water (1.25 C.)

Directions:

1. To start off, grease your bread machine pan. Once this is complete, carefully add in all of the dry ingredients from the list above followed by the liquid ingredients.

2. Once everything is in place, select the proper cycle to cook your cornbread. Depending on the model of bread machine you have, it will say either white bread, quick bread, bake, normal, or basic cycle setting. With the proper setting selected, choose either a light or medium crust color before pressing start.

3. In the last cycle, check the dough consistency. As always, you may need to add more gluten-free flour if your dough is too wet. By the end, the consistency should be slightly wet and thick. Once this is achieved, finish the cycle and cook your cornbread.

4. With the cycle finished, turn your machine off and carefully remove your bread. It may be tempting to eat fresh out of the pan, but allow it to cool, so you don't burn yourself!

Nutritional Information:

Calories: 165

Carbs: 20g

Fats: 9g

Proteins: 5g

Oatmeal Bread

Time: Three Hours

Yields: One and a Half Pound Loaf

Ingredients:

- Rolled Oats (.50 C.)
- Honey (2 T.)
- Salt (1 t.)
- Xanthan Gum (2 t.)
- Potato Starch (1 C.)
- Gluten-free Almond Flour (2 C.)
- Sugar (2 T.)
- Dry Active Yeast (2 t.)
- Baking Powder (.50 t.)
- Apple Cider Vinegar (1 T.)
- Egg Whites (2)
- Olive Oil (.25 C.)
- Warm Water (1.25 C.)

Directions:

1. Before you begin baking your oat bread, be sure that you grease the pan of your bread machine well. When you have completed this task, carefully place all of the ingredients from the list above into your bread

machine. At this point, you will want to leave the oats out.

2. With everything in place, select the proper setting. Depending on your model, it will say either sweet bread, quick bread, bake, normal, or basic cycle. With the proper setting selected, also choose to bake either a light or medium crust color. When you are ready, press start and begin to bake your bread.

3. When the bread is in the final kneading cycle, be sure to check the consistency of the bead. In the final cycle, the dough should be slightly firm but still wet. If needed, add flour or water. Remember that your gluten-free dough is not going to have the same consistency of normal bread dough. When the dough has the consistency desired, go ahead and finish the bread cycle. In the last five minutes, add in the oats and allow the machine to knead until the end.

4. Once the bread is finished, turn the machine off and carefully remove your oat bread from the bread machine. At this point, feel free to add oats on top of the bread for extra flavor. Allow the bread to cool on a wire rack for ten to fifteen minutes before you enjoy.

Nutritional Information:

Calories: 70

Carbs: 14g

Fats: 2g

Proteins: 3g

Onion Bread

Time: Three Hours

Yields: One and a Half Pound Loaf

Ingredients:

- Fat-free Butter (1 T.)
- Onion (1)
- Salt (1 t.)
- Xanthan Gum (2 t.)
- Potato Starch (1 C.)
- Gluten-free Almond Flour (2 C.)
- Sugar (2 T.)
- Dry Active Yeast (2 t.)
- Baking Powder (.50 t.)
- Apple Cider Vinegar (1 T.)
- Egg Whites (2)
- Olive Oil (.25 C.)
- Warm Water (1.25 C.)

Directions:

1. Before you begin baking your bread, you will want to prepare your onion. You will do this by peeling the onion and then slicing it into thin pieces. With his step complete, place a skillet over a low to medium heat. As the pan warms up, add in the tablespoon of

butter and then place the onion. You will want to cook the onion for ten minutes, or until the onion becomes caramelized and a nice brown color.

2. With your onion cooked, you will then want to place all of the remaining ingredients into your bread maker. Be sure you grease the pan well to avoid the bread from sticking to the sides. At this point, you will want to leave the caramelized onion out of the bread maker.

3. Now that all of your ingredients are in place, it will be time to select the proper cooking setting. Depending on your model, it will be white bread, quick bread, bake, normal, or basic cycle. Be sure you also choose either a light or medium crust color at this point as well. When you are all set, go ahead and press the start button.

4. During the final cycle, be sure always to check the dough consistency. You will want a slightly firm dough that is still slightly wet. If needed, add flour or water to achieve this. In the last five minutes of the cycle, be sure to add in the onions you have already cooked.

5. When the cycle is complete, turn the machine off and remove your bread from the pan. Allow the bread to cool, and it will be ready to be served with any meal.

Nutritional Information:

Calories: 105

Carbs: 21g

Fats: 2g

Proteins: 4g

Orange Bread

Time: Three Hours

Yields: One and a Half Pound Loaf

Ingredients:

- Orange Peel (.50 t.)
- Orange Juice Concentrate (3 T.)
- Honey (3 T.)
- Salt (1 t.)
- Xanthan Gum (2 t.)
- Potato Starch (1 C.)
- Gluten-free Almond Flour (2 C.)
- Sugar (2 T.)
- Dry Active Yeast (2 t.)
- Baking Powder (.50 t.)
- Apple Cider Vinegar (1 T.)
- Egg Whites (2)
- Olive Oil (.25 C.)
- Warm Water (1.25 C.)

Glaze Ingredients:

- Orange Juice (2 T.)
- Powdered Sugar (.75 C.)

Directions:

1. Place all of the ingredients from the list above into the greased pan of your bread machine.

2. With everything in place, select the sweet bread, quick bread, bake, normal, or basic cycle setting on your bread machine. Once the proper setting is selected, you should also have the option to create either a light or medium crust color. When everything is set, press start and begin to bake your orange bread.

3. When the bread machine hits the last kneading cycle, be sure always to check the consistency of the dough. Unlike traditional bread dough, the dough for this orange bread should be slightly firm. If it is not, you may need to add flour or water to the dough, one tablespoon at a time. Be sure that the dough is not too firm as your bread will come out tough as a rock!

4. As the bread finishes the cooking cycle, you can prepare your glaze. To do this, all you will need to do is take a small bowl and gently combine the powdered sugar with the orange juice. You will want to continue to stir these ingredients until they are well combined.

5. Once the bread is finished, you can turn your machine off and carefully remove the bread from the pan. I would give the bread ten to fifteen minutes to cool

down. Once it is cool enough to serve, spoon the glaze over the top, slice the bread, and enjoy your treat!

Nutritional Information:

Calories: 175

Carbs: 33g

Fats: 5g

Proteins: 5g

Pizza Bread

Time: Three Hours

Yields: One and a Half Pound Loaf

Ingredients:

- Diced Pepperoni (.50 C.)
- Dried Oregano (1 t.)
- Garlic Powder (1 t.)
- Shredded Mozzarella Cheese (.33 C.)
- Salt (1 t.)
- Xanthan Gum (2 t.)
- Potato Starch (1 C.)
- Gluten-free Almond Flour (2 C.)
- Sugar (2 T.)
- Dry Active Yeast (2 t.)
- Baking Powder (.50 t.)
- Apple Cider Vinegar (1 T.)
- Egg Whites (2)
- Olive Oil (.25 C.)
- Warm Water (1.25 C.)

Directions:

1. To start this recipe, grease up your bread pan and place all of the ingredients from the list above into

your bread machine. At this point, you will want to leave out the diced pepperoni pieces.

2. With everything in place, select the white bread, quick bread, bake, normal, or basic cycle setting. Depending on how you like your pizza, you can choose either a light or a medium crust color. Personally, I like my pizza with a bit of crunch! When you are ready, press the start button and begin the cycle.

3. In the last cycle, be sure to check the consistency of your dough. If the dough is too dry, add water. If the dough feels it's too wet, make an adjustment by adding a tablespoon of flour, add flour. Be sure to complete this step one tablespoon at a time, so you do not mess the dough up further. By the end, the dough should be slightly firm but still wet. With five minutes left in the cycle, you will want to add in the pepperoni pieces.

4. Once the cycle is complete, turn the machine off and carefully remove your pizza bread from the pan. Be sure to allow the bread to cool for ten to fifteen minutes before enjoying. This is one bread the whole family will enjoy and beg you to make again!

Nutritional Information:

Calories: 185

Carbs: 15g

Fats: 5g

Proteins: 7g

Potato Bread

Time: Three Hours

Yields: One and a Half Pound Loaf

Ingredients:

- Mashed Potato Flakes (.50 C.)
- Salt (1 t.)
- Xanthan Gum (2 t.)
- Potato Starch (1 C.)
- Gluten-free Almond Flour (2 C.)
- Sugar (2 T.)
- Dry Active Yeast (2 t.)
- Baking Powder (.50 t.)
- Apple Cider Vinegar (1 T.)
- Egg Whites (2)
- Olive Oil (.25 C.)
- Warm Water (1.25 C.)

Directions:

1. Nothing quite beats warm, delicious potato bread. This bread is perfect to use for sandwiches and to enjoy alongside any meal! To start this recipe, you will first want to grease the pan of your bread machine. When that step is complete, carefully add in all of the ingredients from the list above.

2. Once everything is in place, you will first be selecting the proper cook setting. Depending on your model, it will say white bread, quick bread, bake, normal, or basic cycle. Once the setting is selected, you will also need to decide if you would like a light or medium crust color. When you are ready, go ahead and press the start button.

3. In the last cycle of kneading, you will want to take a few moments to check the consistency of the dough. At this point, the dough should be thick but still slightly wet. If it is not, you will want to add a tablespoon of water or a tablespoon of flour depending on what you need. When you achieve the proper consistency, finish the bread cycle.

4. When the cycle is finished, turn your machine off and carefully remove the bread from the pan. Be sure that you always allow the bread to cool before you handle it.

Nutritional Information:

Calories: 90

Carbs: 17g

Fats: 2g

Proteins: 4g

Pumpkin Bread

Time: Three Hours

Yields: One and a Half Pound Loaf

Ingredients:

- Pumpkin Puree (1 C.)
- Vanilla Extract (2 t.)
- Cream Cheese (.50 C.)
- Salt (1 t.)
- Xanthan Gum (2 t.)
- Potato Starch (1 C.)
- Gluten-free Almond Flour (2 C.)
- Sugar (2 T.)
- Dry Active Yeast (2 t.)
- Baking Powder (.50 t.)
- Apple Cider Vinegar (1 T.)
- Egg Whites (2)
- Olive Oil (.25 C.)
- Warm Water (1.25 C.)

Directions:

1. Pumpkin bread is a wonderful type of bread to be able to bake. This is bread that can be enjoyed during all seasons. The mix of the pumpkin and cream cheese bring out the delicious spices and will be enjoyed by

all. When you are ready to make your own, fresh pumpkin bread, carefully place all of the ingredients into the pan of your bread maker. Be sure you grease the pan down well to avoid any sticking or burning.

2. When all of the ingredients are in place, you will first need to select the proper cooking setting. Depending on your bread machine model it will say white bread, quick bread, bake, normal, or basic cycle. Please also decide at this point if you would like a light or a medium crust color. Once these two choices are selected, press the start button.

3. Once your bread machine reaches the final kneading cycle, pause it so you can check the consistency of the dough. At this point, the dough should be slightly firm and thick. If it is not, use this time to add a tablespoon of water and tablespoon of flour depending on which you need. When you are happy with the consistency, finish the cycle.

4. When the bread machine is done, turn it off, remove the bread and allow cooling for ten to fifteen minutes, and then you can slice it up and enjoy!

Nutritional Information:

Calories: 100

Carbs: 30g

Fats: 14g

Proteins: 5g

Rosemary Bread

Time: Three Hours

Yields: One and a Half Pound Loaf

Ingredients:

- Italian Seasoning (.50 t.)
- Ground Black Pepper (.25 t.)
- Dried Rosemary (1.25 t.)
- Salt (1 t.)
- Xanthan Gum (2 t.)
- Potato Starch (1 C.)
- Gluten-free Almond Flour (2 C.)
- Sugar (2 T.)
- Dry Active Yeast (2 t.)
- Baking Powder (.50 t.)
- Apple Cider Vinegar (1 T.)
- Egg Whites (2)
- Olive Oil (.25 C.)
- Warm Water (1.25 C.)

Directions:

1. When you cook this bread, everyone in your home will be asking where that delicious scent is coming from. Before you begin cooking, you will want first to grease up the pan of your bread machine. Once this step is

complete, you can add in all of the ingredients from the list above into the pan.

2. Once all of your ingredients are in place, select the cycle of baking depending on the model of bread machine you own. It will be the white bread setting, quick bread, bake, normal, or basic cycle. You will also be selecting the crust color at this point, either a light crust or a medium crust. Once done, you can press the start button.

3. During the final kneading cycle of your bread machine, hit the pause button. Take a minute or two to check the consistency of the dough. At this point, it will be firm but still wet. If you feel that the dough is either too dry or wet, make adjustments with water or flour. By the end, the dough should be slightly firm but not rock hard. When you achieve the desired consistency, finish the baking cycle.

4. Finally, turn your machine off and carefully remove the bread from the pan. Allow cooling before you enjoy. This bread tastes wonderful by itself with a smear of butter, or even with your favorite soup!

Nutritional Information:

Calories: 150

Carbs: 25g

Fats: 3g

Proteins: 6g

Chapter Three: Gluten-free Buns and More Recipes

While it is all good and fun to make all different types of bread in the bread machine, it can do so much more! For those who think that a gluten-free diet means a bland diet, you are about to be proven wrong! In the chapter to follow, you will be learning all of the delicious recipes you can make in your bread machine from hot, sticky cinnamon rolls to delicious calzones. Whether you are craving sweet or savory, this cookbook has got you covered!

Bread Sticks

Time: One Hour

Yields: Eighteen Breadsticks

Ingredients:

- Sesame Seeds (3 T.)
- Unsalted Butter (3 T.)
- Salt (1 t.)
- Xanthan Gum (2 t.)
- Potato Starch (1 C.)
- Gluten-free Almond Flour (2 C.)
- Sugar (2 T.)
- Dry Active Yeast (2 t.)
- Baking Powder (.50 t.)
- Apple Cider Vinegar (1 T.)
- Egg Whites (2)
- Warm Milk (1 C.)

Directions:

1. Breadsticks are often a dinner time staple. Now, you can make your own, so you can enjoy breadsticks fresh out of the oven! Before you begin cooking, you will first want to heat your oven to 375 degrees. As the oven warms up, you can also prepare two baking

sheets by lightly spraying them down with cooking spray or oil.

2. Next, you will want to grease your bread machine up and place all of the ingredients from the list above into the pan. When everything is in place, you will select the dough, knead, or manual cycle depending on your bread machine model. When you press start, this will begin to prepare your dough.

3. When the kneading cycle is finished, you will want to place flour on your hands and then carefully shift the dough to a clean working space. Once the dough is in place, gently punch the dough down so that you have a flat surface. When this step is achieved, carefully divide the dough into eighteen pieces. You will want to roll each piece of dough and create a breadstick shape. The best way to achieve this look is to roll the dough from the center to the outside edge.

4. Once you have your breadsticks, you can place them on the baking sheets you prepared already. Be sure that the breadsticks are about an inch apart before you pop the baking sheet into the oven. Once in place, bake the breadsticks for fifteen to twenty minutes. By the end, the crust of the dough should be a nice golden-brown color.

5. When the breadsticks are finished cooking, remove them from the oven and allow cooling before you serve them. Enjoy!

Nutritional Information:

Calories: 85

Carbs: 14g

Fats: 2g

Proteins: 3g

Calzones

Time: Two Hours

Yields: Eight Rolls

Ingredients:

- Salt (1 t.)
- Xanthan Gum (2 t.)
- Potato Starch (1 C.)
- Gluten-free Almond Flour (2 C.)
- Sugar (2 T.)
- Dry Active Yeast (2 t.)
- Baking Powder (.50 t.)
- Apple Cider Vinegar (1 T.)
- Egg Whites (2)
- Olive Oil (.25 C.)
- Warm Water (1.25 C.)

Filling:

- Sliced Mushrooms (.50 C.)
- Sliced Pepperoni (.50 C.)
- Sliced Green Bell Pepper (.50 C.)
- Mozzarella Cheese (.50 C.)
- Pizza Sauce (.50 C.)

Directions:

1. Calzones are the perfect recipe for any family dinner. As you can tell from the list above, I have decided to put green bell peppers, mushrooms, and pepperoni into my calzone. It is fun to make this recipe a group activity and have everyone customize their own calzone! The possibilities are endless! When you are ready to make the calzones, place all of the ingredients from the first list into your bread machine and select the dough, knead, or manual cycle.

2. When the kneading cycle comes to a finish, you will want to place some flour from your hands to avoid anything sticking to you. At this point, carefully transfer the dough to a clean workspace that has been dusted with flour. Once in place, punch the dough flat and allow it to rest for ten minutes or so.

3. As the dough rests, take this time to heat your oven to 400 degrees. As the oven warms up, you can prepare a baking sheet by greasing it down and setting it to the side.

4. Next, you will be dividing the dough into eight pieces. Once separated, you will roll each piece into a six-inch diameter pizza crust. When the pieces are rolled out as desired, spoon a tablespoon of pizza sauce into the

bottom half of the crust and then sprinkle the cheese and whatever fillings you want for your calzone.

5. When you have customized your calzone to your liking, carefully fold the open half over the filled half and create half circles. You will then want to seal the edges of the crust by pinching them together. Once this is complete, you can place your calzones onto the baking sheet and pop them into the oven for thirty to forty minutes. By the end, your calzones will have a gorgeous golden-brown color.

6. Once finished, remove the calzones from the oven, allow to cool, and enjoy!

Nutritional Information:

Calories: 200

Carbs: 20g

Fats: 10g

Proteins: 10g

Cinnamon Buns

Time: Two Hours

Yields: Eight Buns

Ingredients:

- Salt (1 t.)
- Xanthan Gum (2 t.)
- Potato Starch (1 C.)
- Gluten-free Almond Flour (2 C.)
- Sugar (2 T.)
- Dry Active Yeast (2 t.)
- Baking Powder (.50 t.)
- Apple Cider Vinegar (1 T.)
- Egg Whites (3)
- Warm Unsweetened Milk (1.25 C.)
- Unsalted Butter (4 T.)
- Instant Vanilla Pudding Mix (.50 C.)
- Raisins (2 T.)
- Walnuts (2 T.)
- Ground Cinnamon (1 t.)
- Brown Sugar (.75 C.)

Glaze:

- Milk (1 t.)

- Unsalted Butter (4 T.)
- Vanilla Extract (.25 t.)
- Confectioners' Sugar (.50 C.)

Directions:

1. Picture this. You are walking through the mall; the scent of cinnamon rolls fills your senses, and the cravings take over. Now, imagine if your whole house could smell like that whenever you like! This recipe is a simple way to enjoy your favorite treat, gluten-free! It is a win-win situation! When you are ready to start, place all of the cinnamon roll ingredients into your greased bread machine pan, minus the raisins, walnuts, cinnamon, brown sugar, and butter.

2. When everything is in place, you will run the ingredients through the dough, knead, or manual cycle. After you press start, take a few moments to clear a workspace and put down some flour. Finally, place some flour on your own hands and remove the dough from your bread machine when the cycle is complete. When the dough is in your clean workspace, use a rolling pin to shape your dough into one, large rectangle.

3. Next, you will want to take a small bowl so you can mix together the cinnamon, brown sugar, and butter.

Once everything is combined well, spread it over your dough and then top with raisins and walnuts as desired. When this is complete, carefully roll the rectangle into one big log, starting from the widest edge. Once the dough is rolled, pinch the seams so you can seal the roll together. With the roll secure, carefully cut the dough in one-inch slices and then place onto a greased baking sheet. At this point, you will want to allow the rolls at least thirty minutes to rest. During this time, you will notice that the dough will double in size.

4. As you wait for the rolls to rise, heat your oven to 350 degrees. After the proper amount of time has passed, you will pop the baking sheet into your oven for twenty to twenty-five minutes. By the end, the rolls will be warm and golden. With care, remove from the oven and let cool.

5. As the rolls cool, you can prepare your glaze by taking out a bowl and mixing together the milk, butter, vanilla, and sugar. Once the rolls are cool enough, serve the glaze over the top and enjoy!

Nutritional Information:

Calories: 150

Carbs: 25g

Fats: 6g

Proteins: 2g

Challah Bread

Time: Two and a Half Hours

Yields: Two Loaves

Ingredients:

- Salt (1 t.)
- Xanthan Gum (2 t.)
- Potato Starch (1 C.)
- Gluten-free Almond Flour (2 C.)
- Sugar (2 T.)
- Dry Active Yeast (2 t.)
- Baking Powder (.50 t.)
- Apple Cider Vinegar (1 T.)
- Olive Oil (.25 C.)
- Warm Water (1.25 C.)
- Egg Whites (4)
- Sesame Seeds (1 T.)
- Poppy Seeds (1 T.)

Directions:

1. To begin this recipe, you will want to place all of the ingredients from the list above into your bread machine, minus the poppy seeds. Be sure that you grease the bread pan well to avoid any sticking or burning. Once in place, you will want to select the

dough, knead, or manual cycle depending on the model of bread machine you own.

2. Once the kneading cycle has completed, put some flour on your hands and on a clean working space. When you are ready, transfer the dough to the workspace and divide the dough into six pieces. With the six separate pieces, you will want to roll each piece into a log and leave to rest for a few minutes.

3. As the bread is resting, you can heat your oven to 350 degrees. As the oven warms up, it is time to prepare your challah bread. You will do this by pinching the top of the three logs together and then carefully braiding the pieces together. When this is complete, pinch the bottom ends and set onto a prepared baking sheet. You will want to do the same step for the final three pieces of dough.

4. Once the dough is on the prepared baking sheet, place a dampened towel over the top and allow the dough to sit for at least thirty minutes. During this time, the dough should double in size. If not, allow to sit for a little while longer.

5. As the dough rests, you will want to take a small bowl and begin beating the egg whites with a single tablespoon of water. Once this step is complete, you

can carefully brush the egg white mixture over your challah bread. With the egg whites in place, sprinkle the sesame and poppy seeds over the top and pop the baking sheet into your oven for thirty minutes. By the end, the crust should be golden-brown.

6. Finally, remove the bread and let cool.

Nutritional Information:

Calories: 100

Carbs: 15g

Fats: 5g

Proteins: 4g

Naan Bread

Time: Two Hours

Yields: Six Pieces of bread

Ingredients:

- Salt (1 t.)
- Xanthan Gum (2 t.)
- Potato Starch (1 C.)
- Gluten-free Almond Flour (2 C.)
- Sugar (2 T.)
- Dry Active Yeast (2 t.)
- Baking Powder (.50 t.)
- Apple Cider Vinegar (1 T.)
- Egg Whites (3)
- Olive Oil (2 T.)
- Unsweetened Warm Milk (.66 C.)
- Yogurt (.66 C.)
- Unsalted Butter (2 t.)

Directions:

1. To begin this recipe, you will first want to grease the pan for your bread machine. When this is done, place all of the ingredients from the list above and select the dough, knead, or manual cycle. When you press start,

this will prepare the dough. As you wait, you can heat your oven to 500 degrees and prepare a baking sheet.

2. Once the dough is formed, flour your workspace and your hands. Carefully transfer the dough over to your workspace and divide the dough into six pieces. Once this is complete, use a rolling pin to flatten each piece to a third of an inch thick.

3. When you have your pieces of dough rolled out, place the dough onto the baking sheet and then pop the baking sheet into the oven for about ninety seconds. During this time, the bread should puff slightly. At this point, you will want to put your broiler on and toast the bread pieces to a nice golden-brown.

4. At this point, remove the bread from the oven, allow to cool, and enjoy!

Nutritional Information:

Calories: 140

Carbs: 20g

Fats: 5g

Proteins: 5g

Conclusion

I hope at this point in the book, you feel confident and excited to begin baking the gluten-free way. While of course, it is different from the way you have enjoyed food up to this point, you may find this way of cooking even more enjoyable when you realize that you no longer deal with the aftermath of eating the wrong foods.

While it is fun to follow certain recipes, I always encourage creative freedom. If there is an ingredient you don't like in one of my recipes, feel free to switch it out. You may be gluten-free now, but that does not mean you need to eat blandly! Remember, it is great that you are trying gluten-free, but eating healthy doesn't mean that you have to take the joy out of food. There are healthy alternatives out there that are designed to keep you healthy AND at the same time bring you joy as you eat.

Have fun baking and share the joy!

Sierra A. May

Connect with us on our Facebook page

www.facebook.com/bluesourceandfriends and stay tuned to our

latest book promotions and free giveaways.

Made in the USA
Monee, IL
12 June 2020